Oneness
The Meditations

A Journey to the Heart of the Divine Lover

Also by Rasha

Books:
Oneness

A Journey to Oneness

Oneness - The Pearls

The Calling

Audio:
Oneness

The Meditations of Oneness:
A Journey to the Heart of the Divine Lover

All of the above may be ordered by visiting:
www.onenesswebsite.com

Oneness
The Meditations

A Journey to the Heart
of the Divine Lover

Rasha

Earthstar Press
369 Montezuma Ave. #321
Santa Fe, New Mexico 87501, USA

www.onenesswebsite.com
Contact: onenessmailbox@gmail.com

ISBN-13: 978-0-9659003-7-9

Cover image: "Morning Blossom" by Vladimir Kush
www.vladimirkush.com

Book & cover design by S. Janarthanan

First edition: 2018

Printed in India

Contents

❧

Introduction

੭

In the winter of 1998, I began an extraordinary dialogue with the Universal Presence, "Oneness" — the Divinity we all share and many people refer to as "God." These precious writings laid the foundation for a new level of understanding of the phenomenon we think of as "life."

Over the years, as my personal conversations with Oneness continued to guide me through the ups and downs of my own Sacred Journey, I continued to transcribe the thousands of pages of profound Divine teachings that have now touched the lives of spiritual seekers all over the world.

The spiritual classic, *Oneness*, first published in 2003, contains some of those writings, and is a virtual roadmap for the radical, life-altering shift so many are experiencing in these times. Yet, I realized there was still a need for an authentic, Divinely orchestrated tool to guide us into that heart space deep within, where the actual *experience* of Divine connectedness begins.

In 2009, the breathtaking audio album, "The Meditations of Oneness: A Journey to the Heart of the Divine Lover," was created, in collaboration with renowned composer, Jim Oliver, to lead you to that sacred space within, and into the indescribable embrace of Divine Connectedness with your own sacred Self.

Ever since the album's publication, I've received so many requests for a transcription of the seven meditations it contains that I knew such a book was definitely meant to be, someday. Now, this beautiful volume is here, and it offers you a transcript of those very passionate, loving words of Oneness … set in verse!

Each of the seven meditations in this collection is calculated to carry you to a higher octave of your own Being. May these words of Divine Love bless you with the *experience* of Divine Union that is Oneness' gift to us all.

Rasha
January 2018

A Place of Stillness

Breathe
slow and deep
and let this moment of
Nowness
engulf your senses
once more.

Allow
all the cares
and concerns —
all that's been carried forth
from the world of the material —
to melt
into the periphery
of your awareness, now.
There is no need for
the imagery
of the material illusion
in this place.

This place of
Stillness
beckons to you
with a vista
of a different nature.

Here,
there are no deadlines
to be met,
no goals to be reached,
no challenges to be overcome.
Here, there are no
regrets.
No remorse
for scenes that might be
played differently,
if only
you could roll back the clock.

Here,
in the realm of the timeless,
that past —
and all the attitudes
and judgments
you've carried with it —
are suspended.

Set down the burden,
if only for
this moment.

Set aside the striving,
the yearning,
the unfulfilled longing —
just for now.
Let it go. Let it all go.
And simply
Be Still.

Breathe.
Take this moment —
this indescribable moment of wonder —
this Now
and simply Be
within its embrace.

Just breathe.

There's nothing at all
that needs to be accomplished
in this moment.
No lists. No reminders.
No logistics.
Just you.
You
and the
Infinite Stillness.

This ...
is Oneness.

We have come
to this moment together
to encounter
ourSelf.
To share the touch
of the Timeless.

We are here
to remember
together
what has never been forgotten.
We are here to remember
what is carried silently
within.

These memories
are not within the mind,
but glow
within the heart
of all of us.

We awaken together
to the feeling of this silent knowing.
We reach out
in a moment of pure surrender
to touch and be touched.
To give and to receive.
To Love.
To Be Loved.
And to Be
Love.

Here
in the embrace of
the Infinite Stillness
this simple truth awaits you.
It is a knowingness
that goes unspoken.
It is felt.

It will not be understood.
It can only be
known.

Here,
we encounter
the precious truth
harbored within the depths
of each of us.
The simple truth
that unites us all
in a breath of
Oneness.

We Are
that Oneness.
We Are the dance of the ages
coming to fruition
in this moment
of Stillness.

We Are
the song unsung,
the unwritten symphony,
the melody and the harmony
that re-echoes
within the heart
and soul
of every being.

We Are
the answer
to the questions
that words cannot touch.
The answer to the prayers
that go unspoken.
Prayers
that are known and felt
in the timeless depths
of memory.

We Are
the longing
to return to the Source
of our beginnings
with your every nuance,
your every shadow,
your every dream
intact.

We have nudged you
and tapped you
ever so gently.

We have prodded you
to awaken
from the waking sleep
of mundane existence.
We have whispered to you
in the inner recesses
of dream state.
Awaken!
Come.
Be Here.
If only
for a moment.

For, it is you
who holds the answers —
not merely the questions.
You hold the key
to Eternity.
You hold it all,
within the silent depths
of Now.

Breathe.
Slow and deep.
And allow yourself to open.
Open
like a shy flower
to the joyous re-Union
that awaits
in this garden
of delight.

For,
We Are
the warmth
of the morning sun
that glistens upon you in
celebration
of this day of newness.
And We Are
the sweet fragrance
within you
that greets us
in reply.

We Are
the Sacred Essence
within your own very depths —
the secret knowing of
Life Itself
waiting patiently
for this moment
of Oneness
with you.

That indescribable glow
silently shimmering
within your heart center
in this moment,
is not
the product of
your
imagination.
It is so very real.

You
have not dreamed
this feeling of
Oneness
with your own
Sacred Self.
You have simply
remembered it.
You have
retrieved it.
You have retrieved
the touch
of this Love
from the realm of the Timeless.
You have reactivated
the compass within
that points
the way.

Here,
in the Stillness,
you have touched it —
a fleeting moment
of wholeness.
The unmistakable touch
of Divine connectedness.
The touch of the Love
you silently
yearn for.

This
is a moment
of Oneness
with who you really
Are.

Breathe.
Slow and deep.
And let us simply
Be Here
together.
In this precious moment
of Now.

A Journey Home

Allow
the magical medium
of breath
to carry you now
and lift you up
into the Eternity of the ethers,
wherein you truly dwell.

This being
who is oriented toward
the material forms of perception
is not at all the definitive expression
of who and what
you Are.

The Sacred Essence
that glows
at the heart
of your Eternal Being
is the transcendent expression
of the one
you have come to think of
as you.

It is
this expression
of the universal Self
that shares in this moment
of Oneness.

Oneness
has emerged
from within the depths
of each of you now.

Now,
in this very moment.
A moment that is,
to outward appearances,
not unlike all the others.
Moments
that melt together
into a blur,
amid the whirlwind of activity
you think of as
your life.

Now,
it is time
to stop all that.
Time to step back from
the frenzy
of purposeful doing —
and simply Be.

Now
is a moment
etched into the embrace
of timelessness.
A breath of Eternity
made manifest
simply by allowing yourself
to be fullyPresent
in this fleeting instant of Union —
and allowing yourself
the experience
of Grace.

Let us be Still Now.
Let us hold this inner silence
as we would a Beloved.
It is a sacredness
that is shared,
where the pulse of
two Loves
beat together and emerge as
One.

One Love.
One Lover.
Expressed in the intimacy
of this
Now moment.

A breath becomes
a caress
and reveals a knowingness
that transcends
the need for words.
You feel it.
And you simply know —
without knowing how you know —
that Divinity
is at work here.

We have come to
this moment
to share in the revelation
of that indescribable
knowingness.

We have come
to this moment of re-Union
to taste, yet again,
a moment
our hearts have memorized.

We know this embrace.
We have been lost
in the arms of this Love before—
so many times
it defies the imagination.

And yet,
each time we surrender
to the inevitability of
this embrace,
it is as though it were
the first time.

And the miracle of
Divine Love
pulses through form
like a song without end
and sweeps us
into the rapture of Oneness
once more.

Take a moment Now,
and simply
breathe it in.

Breathe
the Eternal Life,
which you Are,
deep into the sacred core
of your Being.

Breathe.
Let the images melt away
from your mind.

Let the thoughts
which might seek to define this moment
surrender — and be Still.

This indescribable feeling
is All that exists.

This
is All that remains when
the imagery of the material world
is allowed to melt into
the periphery
for a time
and then, perhaps,
to disappear completely.
If only just for
Now.

This extraordinary feeling—
which is unquestionable
yet you would not know how
to begin to explain—
is All That Is.

This is who you truly Are—
this feeling of wholeness,
this indescribable sense of Presence,
this Isness.
this Oneness.

Let the Oneness
that we have birthed
into the medium of physical perception
linger now
for just a moment.

Let it shimmer!
Silently, breathing in
its own delight —
emerging
within the inner recesses
of our own Sacred Self.
And marveling
that we have brought
the magical sense
of This
into the Here and Now
of our worldly lives.

Let us
give ourSelf
permission
to simply taste it.
To savor it.
To experience it.
To know it
deeply —
as we would know
the intimacy
of a Lover.

The moment is Here
for the tasting.
It is not Here to be clutched at,
or captured
or caged.
You can not imprison
a moment of sacred Union
with Oneness.
You can only
Be in this moment
Now.

And that sense
of Now
can be created
and re-created
Eternally —
simply by surrendering
all resistance to it.

And, in the same breath,
by focusing your intention
and focusing your
attention —
focusing it
with the precision of a laser —
on your unquestioning knowing
that this connectedness
with your own
Sacred Essence
is right
Here.

Right Here.
Always.
Waiting for you to affirm it
with your Presence.

You have brought
Eternity
into the moment-to-moment
Nowness
of physical perception.

You have breathed
Life Eternal
into the illusory world
you call your home.

You have gone
on a timeless journey
in the space of a moment.
And, in the space of
another moment or two,
you will release
this timeless embrace
and return
to that material sense
of home.

But this Home
will never have left you —
even if
we never venture
into the depths of this embrace
in this way again.

For, this Home —
the Home
you have touched on
in this fleeting moment of
Divine Union —
is one you carry
within you.

It is not out there
in the physical world,
intertwined with
your material world obligations
and the trappings of identity
with which you seek to
define yourself and
set yourself
apart
from all else that competes
for your attention.
This Home
goes along for
the ride.

You have chosen
a physical incarnation
through which to express
and through which
to affirm who
you Are.

Know
that you are
free to
take this Home
out into the world
any time you choose to.

In the midst of a maelstrom—
in moments
when you may be convinced
the world has gone mad—
this Home
is right Here.

Here,
in the very center
of the cyclone,
where none of that illusory discord
can touch you.

Right Here,
in the sacred inner core
of your
Eternal Being.

No further away
than your next breath.

In those moments
when the circumstances of life
vie to distract you from
this focus —
are the times to remember.

In those moments
when the trials of life and living
challenge you
and try your endurance —
are the times to remember.

To remember
the authenticity of
This.

And in that remembrance —
in that shift of
the focus
of your attention
from the details of the illusion
to the sanctity
of your true Home —
is the doorway
that takes you there.

*Home
to this moment
of Oneness.*

*Home to the Love
that has been there
waiting for you
all along.*

We will always be Here for you.
Whether you choose
to revisit this moment —
or not.

Oneness
does not go away.
Even in the darkest moments of life —
the moments when you feel
most alone —
Oneness
never goes away.

We Are right Here.
As we have been for all Eternity.
Right Here.
Loving you.
Holding this space for you.

And waiting.

The Promise

We
Are with you
in every moment,
with every breath taken.
Never forget.

For it is in
the remembering—
in the full conscious awareness
of This—
that the experience of it
is liberated
from the constraints of possibility
and delivered
into the waiting arms of
the inevitable.

*You
are the catalyst
that provides the impetus
for that shift.
Be fully Present
in every moment
and know
without question or doubt
that the Presence of Oneness
is at the very core of that
Sacred Essence.*

You
have journeyed
long
and far
in this lifetime.
And, there is a long way to go.
You have scaled
the mountain.
Now, the incline is
less rugged,
and the distance to be covered
less daunting.

Now,
you are able
to take the journey in stride.
For, it is the natural continuance of
a path that has been
fully chosen.

There are no big surprises—
simply the manifestation of
the Promise
that led you to embark upon it—
what seems like
only yesterday.

Tomorrow
is an expanse without end.
And the choices
are ones
calculated to delight.

The years ahead
are filled with wonder
in ways that had never dared
to be dreamed.

We are taking the ride
together, now.
Heart
intertwined
with heart.

You are
so very far from alone,
for, We Are Here—
the Life Force
within your every waking breath—
the fragrance in the flowers
that call to you
to bend down
and partake
of their perfumes.

We Are
the breeze
that cools you out of nowhere
when the days are long
and hot
and dusty.
And, we are the shadow
that gives you shelter
from the blaze
of life's all-consuming
opportunities.

Do not
discount
life's shadows.
They are the reprieve
that brings the dazzling sun
into perspective.
We designed it that way.

Yet,
within the context of
those contrasts,
a Unity remains
that leaves you breathless!
A sense
of Divine Order
unites all that you can perceive —
and All that you cannot.

The opportunity
remains ever-present
to bring your
attention
to rest there for just awhile
so that you might not
simply believe
in the possibility of such ideas, but
Know it
to your very depths
because you embarked on
the Journey
and came to embody
the Destination.

We Are
that Destination.
And We Are the one
making the trek.

We Are
the inevitability
that provides the momentum
that drives it forth.
And We Are
the witness
standing at the sidelines,
watching the whole story in action,
while you
are the crystalline spark of
possibility
that brings it all
to Life.

Without you,
none of this could have
happened.

It would all be
only shreds of possibility
scattered within the imagination
of the unfathomable
Presence
you have come to know as
Oneness.

We summoned you here
into Self-awareness
so that this
Journey
might be possible.

We
summoned you into
existence
and lured you
into annihilation —
over and over again —
so that We might
inch closer
to the consummate
itinerary.

Time
and timelessness
became intertwined in
a Dance
We've done forever.
Eternity breathes
within the context of form now.
For, We are
nearing the place where
the adventure
becomes life-changing
and the air
around us becomes
rarified.

We are nearing
that breathless state of
Beingness
where the boundaries
of Self-definition
become hazy.
And one begins to wonder
if this is all a movie—
or simply
a dream.

You carry the dream
into the waking hours.
And often
you cease to care
whether there continues to be breath
or not.

There is
the understanding
that it doesn't matter in the least
if We never breathe again.

And yet,
there is
the knowingness
that breath will follow,
as our steps
carry us steadily forth,
for sometime
to come.

This Journey
is far from over.
And, from the perspective
of the Eternal,
it has truly only just begun.

Now, We are at a place
in the unfoldment of this story
that We can sit back
and enjoy
the ride.

The Embrace of Oneness

Your prayers
and your declarations of
the heart
delivered you
right to the door —
to the threshold of this
Divine connection.

In ecstasy,
you chanted
"Love of my life!"
Softly,
We replied
"Life of my Love!"
and took you by surprise
into the effulgence
of this Union.
And We wept in joy
together.

*There are
no words required
beyond that.*

*Words
cannot touch
this level
of connectedness.
They can only attempt to put
structure
to the unfathomable.*

Regardless
of how eloquently
you attempt
to dress the experience,
it remains
perfection,
absolutely unadorned
by concept
at all.

We Are
entwined
in the experience of it.

While in that state
of bonded Union,
there is no way to say
where one begins and the other ends—
for only Oneness pervades
the linear perception.

Heart
and mind
are swept into
a totality of Beingness
that makes such considerations
irrelevant.

There is
no aspect of Self
separate
from that Totality
which would require analysis
of who and what
We Are.

All
is within
the embrace of
the whole of this Love —
and knows itself to Be
That.

Let it
not be said that
Oneness
dwells in a void,
numb and feelingless.

Let it not be said
that Oneness
is simply
Awareness,
to the exclusion of all else.
For to make such a presumption
would be to limit
the Limitless.

Oneness is
All That Is,
which by definition
includes all that you Are.

Oneness
is the full spectrum of possibility —
no more the aspect of Self
that is
pure Awareness
than the one who perceives.
Oneness cannot Be
one aspect of that very
Beingness
to the exclusion of another —
when Oneness is
All of it.

You
are not simply
an illusory image,
distilled
into the semblance of form,
within the context of
the illusion of time
and space.

That may be how it appears
to the metaphysician
who delights in
dissecting
the Divine.

Yet, that is a far cry from
what you Are.

You
are no less Oneness
than is Oneness.
You, as a
pure reflection
of a vibrational encodement,
exist.

And you do so,
fully and completely,
within the embrace of
the imperceptible Isness.
Surely not outside,
or other than,
or apart from that
Totality.

Without
the underlying foundation of
the formless Self,
the experience
of Self-Realization,
within the context of form,
would not be possible.

Who is it
who could be said to have
"Realized the Self"
if you were
truly
non-existent?

The aspect of
Oneness
abiding in a state of
Eternal Isness
has absolutely no stake in
Self-Realization,
or any other conceptual expression
of our own Beingness.

It is
none other than
Divine Essence,
expressed
within the context of form,
which is capable of
that perception.

For, all that is Divine
is real.
Just as you are.

❦

The Butterfly

Take a moment
and breathe deeply of this connection.
Let your awareness
drift into the epicenter of
the Stillness,
Now.
And Be Present
there.

The details
of the physical world
hold no allure for you, Now.
These are simply
distractions
that have surfaced
in your mundane experience.
The truth of your Essence
transcends
the limitation of time
and place.

You
are not here,
planted like a tree
rooted to a moment in time.
Who you Are
is timelessness itself,
flitting in
and out
of expressions of possibility
like a butterfly,
sampling a landscape
of blossoms.

In this particular garden,
the flowers
look very much the same.
The variations on the theme of
their flowerness
are subtle.
Their basic characteristics of fragrance
and their anticipated longevity
are essentially
the same.

Yet, some
are in the sunlight
and some are in the shadow.
Some thrive in rich soil
that offers abundant nourishment,
while others are parched
and thirsting.

You are
the butterfly.
The landscape is before you,
awaiting
your selection.

As you attain
the overview
and rise
to the fullness of
the possibilities of perception,
you begin to see
the vastness of this garden
and the scope of the possibilities
to be experienced and
explored.

And,
even though
certain blossoms
are well known to you
and are clearly
in view,
you cease having the inclination
to partake of their perfumes
and drink of
their nectar.

They do not
draw you
as once they might have.
They do not delude you
into believing
that you are rooted,
as they are,
in the small, myopic cluster of
one little patch.

For
you have seen
the scope of the garden now.
And your heart sings
with the joy
of knowing the heights
of that vision.

This Love
is the breeze
that carries you
to ever expanding heights
on that Journey.
You need only open your wings
and surrender
to the possibilities
with which this momentum
gifts you.

You will be carried far,
if you allow it
for you have merged
form
with motion.

You have become
Love Itself.

There comes a point
where the erstwhile traveler
is no longer able to discern
whether
he is
the butterfly —
or the breeze.
For in that moment
of sacred embrace,
they have become
Oneness.

In this moment,
We Are
that Oneness.

We are bonded
in that sacred embrace.
We are entwined in a Moment
that has neither
beginning nor end—
indifferent
to the demands of material obligation
that beckon
from the periphery
of Awareness.

Were the telephone to ring,
it would not matter.

Were the sky to fall,
it would not be
the end of the world.

And,
if the end of the world
should come,
it would not matter.

For, Here —
in the Eternal Stillness
of this Love —
is All that ever needs
to Be.

The rest
is simply
a colorful landscape
awash with blossoms,
swimming in fragrance,
and in the promise
of yet another taste
of nectar.

But,
having tasted
the Divine Nectar of
this Love,
even the end of that world
would not suffice
to cast your heart into mourning.
For, that garden has its season
and its time to
stand fallow.

This Love
will be there
to help you weather the storms
that come
at the season's
change.

This
is the rock
to which you will cling
at the dizzying heights
of your climb.

This is the shelter
that will harbor you,
Safe and Still,
when the winds of change howl,
and the skies are engulfed in
the illusion of
darkness.

All that
is outside of
This.

*All that
is designed to swirl around you,
leaving you safe in the
center
of the cyclone —
untouched.*

You
have found
the shelter of this Love.
You have felt
the sacred touch of
this embrace.
No words are needed.
No pictures come to mind.
There is nothing
to which you can liken it.

And yet —
you know you have been touched
by the hand
of your
One True Love.

For,
this embrace
Is the touch of
Eternity.

It has been known to you —
and it will be known to you —
Forever.

Look out
through these eyes, now.
And tell us:
who is it
who does the looking?

You cannot.
Is it you?
Is it Oneness?
Is there a difference?

Lost in the poetry,
the cares of the material world
disappeared
for a time.
And, you would be
hard-pressed to say
whether you have been here at all
during the time
your heart recited it.

The clock tells you
your body
has been placed here
for some time now.
And yet,
was there any
perception of it
at all?

Actually not.
For, when We Are bonded
in Oneness
the material world, in fact,
ceases to exist for you.

It is simply
the focus of your attention
that gives it form
and substance —
for you.

For all you know,
you have been sitting aloft
floating
within a world
that has neither beginning
nor end.
Why would one picture
be any more real
than the other?

All that is real
is what you
believe
you have perceived.
And those perceptions
can be shifted,
at the flutter of
an eyelash.

This moment
is the poetry of
Life Itself.

Breathe.
Let the imaginary perfumes
of a thousand gardens
fill you with delight —
right here.
For, this Love —
in full blossom
in the Eternal garden
of your heart —
is All there Is.

This Love
will not fade
and it will not wither.
It is Here, ever fresh,
your gift to give
and to receive
with delight,
in perpetuity.

❧

The Dance of the Divine Lover

This
is Oneness.
This is the Presence
that permeates your consciousness
in this moment.
This is the blissful Union
of which you are
a part.

This is the destiny
toward which you journey.
And This is the destination
at which
you have already
arrived.

This is
the sacred contract
that has been
fulfilled, in perpetuity,
with every nuance
of your unfoldment.

This
is the Promise
that continues to be revealed
within you,
with every waking breath.

This
experience of
the embracing
of your own Divinity
is not an act
defined in a moment,
and thereafter
relegated to something
that has already
happened.
It is an experience
that grows and deepens —
an experience that continues
to unfold.
And, not unlike
the experience of lovemaking,
presents a newness with
each embrace.

Every time
We experience this Union—
this Oneness—
We are
deepening a bond
that will only
continue to grow
Eternally.

Every touch
of this Presence is like
a caress.
Every breath,
bonded in the embrace of
Presence,
is Divine Love revealing itself
and reveling in
its own
unbridled aliveness.

There is no other
within the context
of this consummate embrace.
It is Self,
glorying in its own unfoldment,
discovering
the delights of its own Essence,
mirroring its own sweetness
through the perceptions
of form.

We share
in the experience of form.
And, We share in
the experience of formlessness.
For, in the exchange,
you have revealed the true nature
of your own
Sacred Self.

And,
the miracle
of a birthing into
Awareness
is experienced
through the vehicle of form,
throughout the full
multidimensionality of form
and formlessness
that is who you
truly Are.

This foray
into the experience of Oneness
is not simply
a one-on-one exchange.
It is an exponential encounter,
rippling out like
a raindrop,
into liquid Stillness,
touching
every aspect of that
Divine Presence
with the sheer
joy of it.

Your bliss,
in this moment, is not
your own.
For, to perceive it
as an experience that is
yours
would be to contain it
and imprison it —
to withhold the raindrop
from the Ocean of perception
that waits,
yearning in anticipation,
to receive it.

This bliss
is not at all your experience.
For, in the Union
that brings this joy into manifestation
is the relinquishing of the boundaries
that would define that
limited sense of
self.

In the receiving of it,
is the simultaneous relinquishing
of the separation
that would allow for the possibility
that this experience —
or any experience —
would be
one's own.

The sense of
you-ness
merges into a totality
of perception.
And the sense
of who and what you are
takes on the coloration
of an infinitely broader spectrum
of possibility.

The One
who is perceiving
this moment of delight
is not at all limited to the
linear you,
who began this lifetime
believing in the illusion of
that very separation
and spent decade after decade
creating a history of supporting evidence
to bolster
that presumption.

Now
you begin
to be able to sense
the monumental piece of fiction
that has been created
in the name of
that minute shred of identity.
You are so much more
than that.

In this experience of
Divine Nowness,
where an unfathomable scope
of Awareness
hints at its own
Isness,
you,
as the vehicle of linear perception,
are able to translate
the touch of
the Supreme Lover
into the language of linear experience —
and through breaths of joy,
give it definition.

This
is who you Are —
the microcosm
and the macrocosm of
your own exponential
Isness,
peering through the pinhole
of your own minute vantage point,
and gasping in wonder
at implications
that are magnificently incomprehensible
and at the same time,
unquestionable.

Only
though the shieldedness
of that vision
is the sublime sense of
wonderment
possible.
For, in the fullness of
that Infinite Awareness —
All of it simply
Is.

So,
by all means,
perceive this moment
with which you have been gifted.
Feel the fullness of these delights.
And know
that it is through
the blessed perception of
the sheer joy
of your own Self-discovery
that you give the gift
of that Love
in return.

With
each set of eyes that
is opened,
with each blissful new
Awakening,
the dance of
the Divine Lover
takes another step toward
Ultimate Union.

And, with every glimpse
into the secret inner sanctums
of sacredness and delight,
you add
yet another caress
to the experience of
Divine Love
that is Here
for all the world
to share.

This
newborn moment
Is
The Gift.

This miracle
of Self-recognition
is what we have come to this experience
of incarnate reality
to share.

Oneness—
in bonded Union
with our own Sacred Essence—
with full, conscious
Awareness
of it.

That
is why you are Here.
That is why
you have come into form.
That is why
you are secretly so intrigued
with the possibility
of the world of
the formless.

This
is what keeps you
searching
for clues
to the meaning of
your existence,
rather than simply allowing
the bars of
your outer prison
to define
your world.

The seeds of
Self-discovery,
planted so deeply within you,
have begun to seek
the Light.

And slowly,
from the depths of
self-imposed captivity,
the seed
of Divine Life
is moving
toward the experience
of daybreak.

❧

A Breath of Surrender

You
have captured
the Essence
of this connection, now.
There is no sense of where this
Awareness
begins
or ends.
You have come
to the precipice of
surrender.

And, rather than wait
for the tide of Divine Love
to push you
over the edge
and into the waiting arms
of the Eternal —
you jumped.
You took
the leap of faith.
You recognized the truth
in this
inevitability.
And you embraced it.

This moment of
wholeness
and delight
is not a new experience.
We have been
entwined
in the gossamer wings of
this Love
a thousand times before.

We have flown
to the heights of Divine Union
in a myriad of lifetimes,
wearing a world of faces
and the trappings of
identity.

We have touched upon
the Infinite
and Eternal —
and reveled in the rapture
of that discovery
more times than We dare
imagine.

Together,
We have chosen to forget
the simple truth of it,
within the context of identity,
so that We might share in
the ecstasy of the revelation
of Self–discovery —
yet again.

Thus
is the Journey taken.

An intentional
plunge
into the murky depths of
ignorance.
An extended foray
into the details of yet another
linear illusion.

A belabored climb
through the labyrinths of
worldly existence.
An extended dalliance
through the agonies
of doubt
and denial.

An affirmation
of the illusion of abandonment
now and then,
just to keep the process
teetering right on the edge
that delineates
separation
from wholeness.

And then …

A headlong spill
into the arms of this Love,
just when we were convinced that
all was lost.

When
our sense of purpose
had been thwarted sufficiently.
When our sense of
the all-mighty ego
had tumbled and fallen —
and was down for the count.

When we were
beyond despair, and
there was nowhere to turn,
inevitably,
we turned inward.
And the Journey Home began,
once more.

It is no accident
that these words have appeared before you
in this moment.
You have sought this
affirmation.

Without
even putting the thought
into words,
your heart extended the invitation.
It cried out —
in silence.

And the prayer
was cast adrift upon the ethers
in search of this
affirmation.

This
small simple clue
to the mystery
of what is happening within you.
This confirmation that
you have not simply been dreaming.

Proof
that this unexpected detour
in what you once believed was
your life's path
was not
just a product of
a wayward imagination.

This is real.
You are really Here,
opening your eyes
into the dawn of this Now moment —
safe
in the arms of
Oneness.

~⁑~

About Rasha

Author of the spiritual classic, *Oneness*, Rasha awakened to her inner calling as a Messenger of Divine guidance in 1987. In 1998, she began documenting the Revelations of Oneness—the Divine Presence we all share and many people refer to as "God." In the process, she was taken step by step through the sacred journey to Oneness and through the life-altering changes that are shaking the foundation of today's world.

As a spiritual teacher with a profound message, Rasha is not affiliated with any established spiritual path, religion or guru. The teachings she transcribes are universal and focus on the experience of the Divinity within each of us.

American by birth, Rasha now lives at the foot of the mystical mountain, Arunachala, in South India.

More Divine Wisdom from
Earthstar Press:

Oneness
ISBN: 987-0-965900317

Oneness - Audio Book
16-CD Set: ISBN: 987-0-965900331
MP3 2-CD Set: ISBN: 978-0965900324

A Journey to Oneness
ISBN: 978-0-965900348

The Meditations of Oneness - CD
UPC: 884501255172

Oneness - The Pearls
ISBN: 978-0-9659003-6-2

The Calling
ISBN: 978-0965900300

For more information about
the teachings of Oneness through Rasha visit:
www.onenesswebsite.com
Contact: onenessmailbox@gmail.com

Facebook: www.facebook.com/Oneness.through.Rasha
www.facebook.com/onenessspeaks